"Alone, alone, all, all alone;/Alone on a wide, wide sea."

(*Ancient Mariner*, Samuel T. Coleridge)

Collier Books
Macmillan Publishing Company
New York

Collier Macmillan Publishers
London

by Theodore Isaac Rubin, M.D.

□

Jordi

A COMPOSITE CASE HISTORY

Collier Books
Macmillan Publishing Company
866 Third Avenue, New York, N.Y. 10022
Collier Macmillan Canada, Inc.

Library of Congress Cataloging-in-Publication Data
Rubin, Theodore Isaac.
    Jordi / Theodore Isaac Rubin. — 1st Collier Books ed.
        p.   cm.
    ISBN 0-02-053580-5
    1. Schizophrenia in children—Case studies.   I. Title.
RJ506.S3R82   1988
618.92'8982—dc 19   87-37506
                                                                      CIP

Macmillan books are available at special discounts for bulk purchases
for sales promotions, premiums, fund-raising, or educational use.
For details, contact:

                    Special Sales Director
                    Macmillan Publishing Company
                    866 Third Avenue
                    New York, N.Y. 10022

FIRST COLLIER BOOKS EDITION 1988
First printed by Macmillan Publishing Company in 1960

10 9 8 7 6 5 4 3 2 1

Printed in the United States of America

For Ellie

Preface

There is no "Jordi." But in my work I have come to know Jordi's of all ages. I thank them for so many things. They inspired this book, indeed helped compose it. They enhanced my growth, both professionally and personally, and above all they have allowed me to share their experiences. Together we've made some wonderful voyages from darkness to light.

I have endeavored to write a book which is scientifically correct. However, the main endeavor of the book is to convey the feeling, panic, suffering, and tragedy involved in mental disturbance and more explicitly in childhood schizophrenia. Disturbances of this nature are, at best, poorly understood illnesses.

There is a new trend in psychiatry, the establishment of day hospitals, day centers, and day schools for seriously disturbed people. I feel this is a warm, human, healthy approach to a most difficult problem. I would like to congratulate Dr. Carl Fenechel, director and founder of the "League School for Seriously Disturbed Children." Carl Fenechel is indeed a pioneer, engaged in a noble constructive task. His effort will shed much light on this important new approach to the management of very disturbed children.

A special thanks to Florence Stiller—a warm human being—a great friend. Her encouragement, criticism, and "being there" helped me every inch of the way.

Thanks to Nat Freeman, who made it all possible, and my wife Ellie. Her work has not only largely inspired this book, but she has also helped me immeasurably with its technical aspects.

The End

He ran through the train yelling wildly, and nobody heard him. He was alone in the crowded subway and felt that he had to get to the first car before the next station. He tried squeezing between people's legs, but they didn't budge. Much as he struggled, he went unnoticed.

He sat up in bed. The room was dark, and he had to get to the front of the train. Quickly he put on his shirt and trousers and ran quietly out of the house to the IRT. He had several tokens from previous trips. With some difficulty he pushed through the turnstile and was surprised to see nobody on the platform. Funny, how crowded the station and train could be one minute and empty the next —but this didn't bother him.

Three

He rode from Flatbush Avenue to Van Cortlandt Park—standing in front and watching each station's light and warmth reach out to him through the blackness of the tunnel. He knew the stations by heart. They were really old friends—the only friends he ever had.

On the trip back, he fell asleep, leaning against the glass of number one car again.

At Flatbush Avenue the conductor shook him and asked, "What in the world are you doing on the train four o'clock in the morning?"

He pulled away from the big man and ran out of the train, screaming and crying. In no time at all he was home again and in bed.

□ □

He woke up suddenly, looked around the room, and jumped out of bed. People were talking in the kitchen. The woman's voice was high-pitched, tremulous, and sounded very angry. The man's voice said, "Yes—OK, already, OK," and then the door slammed and it was quiet again. He felt like eating but was afraid to go into the kitchen. The garbage pail under the sink, with its greasy, gaping, smelly hole frightened him awfully.

Shaking miserably, he finally opened the door and walked into the room backward. The woman shook her head and said, "Why can't you walk like all of us, Jordi?" He couldn't answer—the pail might hear him. The big hole was like an ear, and it could hear everything—sometimes even his thoughts. If he kept quiet and thought nothing, maybe he could shut it out and make himself safe.

He gulped down his orange juice and ran out of the house. He made it—he was safe again—but he had to be careful of the garbage pails on the street.

And then he remembered that he forgot his jiggler. He had to have his jiggler if he wanted to get by the garbage cans safely. He knew that he had to face the woman again. She just couldn't understand why he wouldn't talk. Sometimes she hugged and kissed him. Sometimes she gave up and shook him.

He marveled at her fearlessness. She talked in front of the can, even picked it up and shook it. But her voice—when that voice got loud and angry, the whole room shook. It felt like he would be crushed by it. It went through him and made him shake and scream inside—stop, stop, stop, stop, stop, but her voice would go on. Sometimes, though, the man's voice, which was kind of deep and smooth, would say, "Stop," and her voice stopped.

He tiptoed into the house, but she saw him and said, "God, Jordi, walk like the rest of us." He took the doorknob attached to a long string and ran past her out of the house. He had his jiggler and was now truly safe.

He let the jiggler hang down in front of him and waited. Soon it would tell his feet where to go. Funny, how his feet followed the jiggler without his even thinking about them. He walked and walked and felt that he was all alone even though there were people here and there.

His feet finally came to the jiggler's destination. There it was—a water tower, very high—sitting up there in the clouds, alone and quiet. He looked at the tower, and it made him feel good inside. He stared at it for a long time, and then the jiggler reminded him that he had to go home again.

All the way home he thought of water towers, flagpoles, high buildings, trees, and many things much taller than he was. Before he knew it, he and his jiggler were in the kitchen eating lunch. Her voice asked if he had a nice walk, and he nodded yes. She kissed the top of his head lovingly, and he said, "It was high—so high, so beautiful."

"What was high? What, Jordi?"

But he was quiet and didn't feel like talking again.

□ □

It rained that morning. He liked the lightning, and the thunder was rumbly and warm. It was the rain that scared him. Every time it came, the same thought was there—rain forest—and it would repeat over and over again—rain forest, rain forest—and the same picture popped into his head—only lately he was more and more in the picture.

The trees were raining down. They weren't the tall, nice ones. They were short, fat, heavy, and stubby. They had giant roots—that spread out all over. And they came down from the sky to look for him, and one day one would come—the one that hated him most. It would crush him into the dirt. The roots would strangle him. He would be buried deeper and deeper.

Jordi jumped out of bed screaming, "Let me go, let me go! I'm choking, choking!" He was out of the house now—

in the street, lying on his back—he clawed the air, gasping for breath.

The neighbor from next door said, "The kid is having a fit." Jordi didn't hear her—the trees were raining down.

□□

The days and nights passed. There were the quiet, safe times—the withdrawn hours. And there were the terrors, the seconds of panic. Sometimes they stretched out into hours, and even days.

□□

He walked out of the house dangling his jiggler before him. He waited for directions. Three boys passed him. They were bored. One said, "Let's have some fun with that queer-looking kid."

One of the other boys grabbed the jiggler and began to swing it around in a wide arc.

Jordi was frozen to the spot. A piece was torn out of his middle. He watched the jiggler go round and round. He felt his head whirl. He didn't even feel the other two boys pushing him. He didn't hear their taunting words. His agony was too great.

And then he began to scream. He didn't hear his own

Seven

voice. He screamed and screamed and paused only to gasp for breath.

The boy dropped the jiggler and ran, and the other two followed. Jordi's mother ran down the stairs, hugged him to her, and picked up the jiggler. They walked upstairs with his head pressed against her belly.

He couldn't stop moaning. The gaping wound was still there. She put him in his bed, washed his face, kissed him and hugged him. After she placed the jiggler in his hand, he fell asleep, exhausted.

□ □

He listened to them talking and knew that it was all about him. He was curious but not really interested. The sounds, and the feelings that they conveyed, moved him somewhere deep inside. The words, however, were just nothing.

The woman's voice was full of tears. "What shall we do, Dan? Where? What school? None will have him. . . . I love that kid so, Dan. He's so helpless. . . . Where did we hurt him? How?"

Jordi lost interest and fell asleep. He was part of his dream now and could not hear his father weeping. He was on a train, all alone. He came to many stations full of light and high towers. There were no people, noise, or garbage cans. He slept soundly.

Eight

The sunlight woke him. The same mean trick had been played on him again. From his very own world he was plunged again into this hated place; people, garbage cans —big ones, little ones. If he could only remain as when his eyes were closed all day like at night—but they all had a way of getting close to him.

And he couldn't shut them out. There were times when he ran and ran, and there were times when he swung his jiggler furiously—but they were still there. Their voices were all around him. And sometimes the voices were there by themselves. And they yelled at him, chided him, prodded him, and he was afraid—he was so afraid—and there was no place to go, no one he could trust.

□

Irene and Dan visited the state institution. They knew there was no choice, but they couldn't bring themselves to commit him. The place looked so forbidding, they felt so hopeless. Their little boy, their first born, their Jordi in Brooksville. They tore at themselves and at each other. But the grim fact stuck. No other place would have him.

And then the letter arrived. Mrs. Harris, the last of a multitude of psychiatric social workers they had consulted, informed them that a special school had been organized. She warned them, however, not to be too optimistic. The school would accept only a handful of children—and these only after much testing, interviewing, and screening. The principal prerequisite had to be fulfilled. In order to be admitted a child had to be severely disturbed—in fact, psychotic.

Eleven

Jordi was observed for hours. There were rooms with one-way mirrors and interviews and tests of all kinds. He played with blocks, ink blots, and little statues of children and adults. The doctors examined him physically as well as mentally. The final diagnostic summary of tests, reports, and interviews read as follows:

"This eight-year-old white, sandy-haired, blue-eyed boy is slightly smaller than his stated age would indicate. ENT are normal. Chest is clear, and heart and circulatory system are normal. Neurological examination is negative. Complete physical examination reveals no system pathology or evidence of organic defect of any kind.

"This child is only moderately oriented in time, place, and person. He apparently suffers from severe anxiety—panic attacks, hallucinatory phenomena—and at times is autistic. Contact is possible but tenuous. There is an obvious thought disorder in evidence. Although there is at times severe intellectual blocking, there is nevertheless evidence of a superior I.Q. and good intellectual potential. The opinion of the diagnostic staff is that this child is suffering from a severe psychotic reaction, undoubtably schizophrenic in nature.

"Final diagnosis: Schizophrenic reaction—type: mixed, undifferentiated, chronic."

Jordi had passed the entrance examination. He was admitted to the school.

The Middle

They led him out of the house into the bus. It was very different from the trains and their routes that he knew so well. Then they went out of the familiar neighborhood.

He was afraid to sit, and nobody objected to his standing the whole way. He felt very small. It made him feel a little bit bigger to stand. He kept his fist clenched tightly on the seat, and his body became more rigid. As familiar surroundings disappeared, he clenched the seat even tighter, feeling that this would keep him from disappearing too.

He felt that if he held himself tightly and didn't budge, he would not come apart. It took immense concentration to hold himself together. Each bump and jolt threatened to make him scatter into little pieces. A private battle was taking place between him and the lurching of the bus.

The attendant talked to him. He didn't answer. He couldn't hear her. Keeping himself in one part absorbed him totally. All of his senses were concentrated on the terrible effort.

He was aware that they were no longer moving. The scene outside the window was a new one. He did not want to step into this scene. The handle of his seat in the bus was his grip on himself. He couldn't let go—he would surely lose himself.

He heard them reasoning and pleading, but he felt that theirs were foreign voices. He couldn't understand their strange language. If they could only go back—back so that he and his jiggler could become themselves again. And then he knew he was saved. He remembered his jiggler. He reached in his pocket and squeezed it.

Friend, friend—lovely, lovely jiggler, he thought.

He felt the strength and wholeness return to him. The jiggler chased the shakiness right out of him.

He was still afraid, but he squeezed the jiggler and felt connected to the old scene. He walked off the bus. The jiggler felt like it hooked the new scene to the old one. He told himself that this was just a part of the places he knew—not a new place—really a newer part of the old place. That way he wasn't new either. That way he remained himself—Jordi.

But when he saw the building, his stomach felt funny. He wasn't so sure now. Holding his jiggler tighter made him feel better. Then he realized he knew the building. This was the place where he fooled with the ink people.

Only this time she wasn't there. She stayed at home. He remembered the doctor listening to his chest. He couldn't go in. He trembled. He wanted to run. The streets, crisscrossing wherever he looked, were like a big puzzle he could get caught in. The bus—the bus—the bus. Where was it? Where, where? He charged into it and shrank into the back seat. He clutched the jiggler so tightly his hand became numb. And then he knew he was dying.

He thought, dead, dead—spread—spread. They fit together. And so it was so. He would soon be dead. Spread—dead—dead spread, he thought. He waited for it to happen. He felt his arm become numb, but he was no longer jumpy. The deadness also brought calmness. The panic was gone, and he waited to die.

But then they were in the bus talking to him. He paid no attention. Dying occupied him completely. Then he realized that they were gone. But now a tray of food was on the next seat, and he forgot to die. He was too busy eating, and the bus felt good. After all, it was connected to the old place.

Now and then he saw a stranger come in. But no words were spoken.

After a while the bus was full again, and in motion. This time he sat comfortably the whole trip. The bus felt warmer—kind of cozy and safe.

He looked around and watched the strangers. He held his jiggler all the time but didn't take it out of his pocket.

He noticed the stranger next to him. Then he looked at the one next to that one. After he looked at them all, he felt a little bit better. But he still wanted to stop being with them. They were still strangers.

He concentrated on the big man behind the wheel. He

remembered the man on the train. Only this man sat; the others walked up and down.

Then he saw the water tower—his very own water tower. There it was, out the window. He got up and ran to that side of the bus. At the same time he yelled, "Hi, tower, high tower—my tower."

In no time at all the bus was parked in front of his house. He jumped out eagerly. She was there to hold him and hug him.

He looked around. Nothing had changed.

He was home from his first day at school.

He drank his milk slowly, watching her as she did the dishes.

Then she asked, "How was it, Jordi?"

"The man was the same on the train."

"What man?"

"The man who sat."

"Who sat, Jordi?"

"The big stranger."

"But how was school, Jordi?"

"School, pool, fool, tool. So jiggle, jiggle."

He took the jiggler out of his pocket and left the house.

The sun was going down, and he felt cold. He went back to the house and put on his sweater. Then he dangled the jiggler and waited.

The jiggler took him all over the neighborhood. He

checked all the places—the tower, the busy street, the subway station. All of it was like before.

Then it was dark, and he felt the jiggler lead him home.

After supper he was very tired. He went to his room and soon fell asleep.

He dreamed that he went to his stations, but, instead of a train, he was on a bus. It was warm and nice. And the stations were nice too. And the big sitting man wasn't a stranger. But then they came to a big empty building. He looked inside and could see it was cold. He heard her say, "Jordi—Jordi, school, school," and sat up fully awake.

He waited for the bus full of strangers to arrive. He heard her voice go up and down. It felt good hearing it close to him that way. But he paid no attention to what it said.

He picked up the dried-out leaf and examined it carefully. Then he traced the veins and their branches between his thumb and forefinger. After a while he rolled it into a ball and crushed it, watching the powder blow away before it reached the ground. Then he picked up a green leaf and tried the same thing. But it turned into a green mash, and his fingers got sticky with its juice. When he licked them, he was surprised at the bitter taste and made a funny face. He heard her voice say, "What's the matter, Jordi?"

And he said, "Nothing, just leaf fingers."

Then the bus arrived, and this time he went in and sat down.

He felt funny with the strangers, and his stomach felt uneasy when the bus left the old neighborhood. Then he recognized a few of the faces. When he saw the same man driving, he thought, train man, and the bad feeling left.

He looked out of the window. It felt as though the streets were rushing by him as he sat still. Then he thought of them as flat boats, and the road became an ocean. Their decks carried many interesting objects, all passing by so he could see them. He felt very important and watched the passing boats carefully. There were all kinds and sizes of people. There were carriages. Then he saw a black cat, and he turned it into a panther. The bus carried him away from the scene just as the panther was about to eat up one of the children.

He felt kind of filled up, puffed out, and lifted. Then suddenly the importance just poured out. It was as though a hole had been punched in the middle of him. The stuff just bled out, and he could feel himself shrinking. And then he felt small, and weak and scared again. They had stopped, and there it was. The big red ink building. He felt the coldness of the doctor's stethoscope again, and knew that it was cold inside.

He watched them all leave the bus. Even the train man left. Then he saw them go into the building. He sat and watched and wondered if they would be frozen by the coldness inside. Then he thought of the building—an ice building, all ice inside.

He thought of ice cubes, and his mother cracking them. He pictured the people walking around in there, cold and stiff. Then he thought of them bumping into each other, and pieces cracking off them like ice cubes.

But then he saw the train man leave the building. He watched him walk down the street. He was surprised to see that he walked quickly and softly, without being stiff at all.

Then he saw somebody look out the doorway at him. He quickly turned his head to the other side, but she didn't

Twenty

look stiff either—even soft. He looked back. No—she really didn't look frozen. Then she disappeared inside.

He took his jiggler out, and let it hang between his legs. It pointed to the door. He followed it. He kept following it. Then he looked up and realized he was out of the bus. He was in the new scene. First he wanted to run back to the bus. But then the sun came from behind a cloud, and the street looked bright and warm like other streets he knew.

He walked around the block several times. When he passed the ice house, a stranger waved to him from the window—but he didn't wave back.

The jiggler took him all over the block. Then he walked through the adjoining streets. He looked at the brownstone houses, and they seemed old and tired to him. Then he came to a busy street—full of stores, traffic, and people. For a while he watched a man wash the windows of a five-and-dime store. Then he walked on and came to an IRT subway station. He went down the stairs, looked the platform over, and then came back into the sunlight.

He covered the whole area three times. Then he went back to the ice house. Now the streets were not so new, and he felt better. But the bus was gone. He looked up and down the street—but no bus. He began to feel very frightened. Then he thought of the subway station two blocks away and felt the shakiness stop.

Then the lady stranger brought a sandwich and milk out to him. She sat near him on the stoop, but he paid no attention to her. He just ate his lunch and thought about the subway station.

And then the rain started. He pictured the rain trees and shuddered. This time he heard her when she said, "Come in, Jordi. Come in out of the rain."

Twenty-one

He was afraid to walk any farther. He leaned against the wall and thought, it isn't an ice house; it isn't. It isn't an ice house; it isn't, it isn't an ice house.

But he couldn't go in. Then the girl came into the hall and said, "Come. Come with Lisa—Lisa–Muriel. Come, come."

He stared at her but didn't budge.

Then she said, "Aw, come on; come on, kid. John, the kid won't come. He won't come, ho hum—ho hum, the kid won't come."

The rhyme interested him. He muttered, "Ho hum, ho hum—won't come, won't come."

She lost interest, though, and disappeared into the room. Forgetting his inhibitions, he walked through the hall to the edge of the room. He could see the whole room now but stopped short. He wanted to go in but just couldn't. Then he began to rock up and back from foot to foot—left to right, right to left. It was almost as if he had to dissipate the energy of his indecision by means of this constant to-and-fro rocking.

The room was very big, with lots of windows and lights. There were all kinds of colored pictures on the walls and a great big blackboard on one side. Then he saw an open closet and all kinds of toys and game boxes sticking out. In the center of the room was a big table with pencils, papers, and crayons on it. Along one side there were several low tables. There were little and big strangers here and there. One stranger looked at him the whole time. And then he remembered her—she was the same one who looked at him through the window when he walked around the block.

Twenty-two

Then the Lisa–Muriel girl stranger came over to him again.

"Come in, kid, come in.

"John," she yelled to her teacher. "John."

A big man stranger came over. "Yes, Lisa, what is it?"

"This kid, this iddy bid kid, won't come in."

"He will when he's ready to, Lisa. When he's ready, he'll come in with his teacher."

"Who's his teacher, John, who? Not you, John, not you."

"Not me, Lisa. Sally is his teacher—Sally over there," he said, pointing at the woman still standing close to Jordi.

Teacher, teacher, Jordi thought. Teacher stranger—strangers, the public—a public, stranger teacher.

He looked at the woman a second but then got interested in Lisa again. But she no longer knew he was there. She was busy now, alternately hopping and skipping around the room. Periodically she let out a whoop and said, "Muriel, Muriel isn't my name, but to me it's the same, the same, the same."

Then a funny thing happened. He saw a picture of the Eiffel Tower on the adjacent wall. He ran over to it and into the room and yelled, "A tower, a tower!"

The woman stranger—the Sally one—sat down in a chair next to him while he looked at the travel poster hanging on the wall.

□ □

The smell of the place was strong and clean. It felt exciting and new. But the unfamiliarity made him feel funny in his stomach. It was like breathing something other than air—heady, strange, and somewhat frightening.

She seemed that way to him too. She was new and fresh, but different. She did the same thing day after day. She met him at the bus, walked inside with him, and was there. Wherever he went, she was there. Whatever he did, she was there. For a long time they said nothing to each other and never touched each other. But—no matter what—there she was, close to him. They were inseparable from the time he got off the bus in the morning until he left for home in the late afternoon. After a while he couldn't shut her out.

After a long time, a change took place. This change was subtle and slow. Jordi was not aware of its happening. But their relationship had changed. He no longer felt that she was separate from him. She and he were one. They had merged—the boundaries of their separate skins were no longer a barrier. And yet a thin line separated the her part of him from the rest of him. Her, she—that part was different; it was with different feelings—warm and soft—but very solid.

And then they began to talk.

□ □

At first their conversation was limited to one or two words.

She would say hello, and he would reply with a timid hello.

And after a while they called each other by name. He kind of liked the name Sally.

And gradually their talking became more complicated. There were more words, and with the words more understanding and feeling passed between them.

□ □

He couldn't stand the new feeling. It got stronger and stronger and then would leave. When it was gone, he felt nothing—just flat. But the feeling would come again, and he felt torn apart from inside by it. He walked on the street near the school with her. The feeling hit—his heart beat wildly. He grabbed her hand.

"Sally. Sally, garbage cans—cans, cans. Sally, please—over again. Ears, ears—hear me—hear me. Cans—please—please."

She walked to the can in front of the school. She kicked it savagely; her face was contorted with anger. She stomped it—and cursed it—and held his hand all the time.

"Hit it, Jordi. Hit it—kick it. Kick it—come on, Jordi. That god-damned can—let's kill it, Jordi."

Jordi felt his head exploding. He jumped on the can—he screamed wildly—he stamped up and down. The can was almost completely flat—there was no hole left. He stopped yelling—calmed down. There was no new feeling now—and no flat one either.

"Sally. Sally, no can—no can—no ear. It's gone. I made it go—I made it go."

"You were angry, Jordi—angry, angry. Remember, Jordi, you were angry."

Jordi muttered to himself, "Angry, angry. I was angry."

The word was familiar—but now the symbol, the meaning, and the feeling were closer to being one. Jordi played with the word for days—tasted it, chewed it up, tested it. "Angry, angry. Sally—I was angry."

□ □

She hit him with her fist. Then she pulled his shirt and kicked his ankle. She yelled in a high-pitched voice, "Louse, louse, leave Lisa alone, alone. Lisa wants to go home now. Lisa wants the crayons—louse, louse."

She kicked his ankle again and again.

Jordi couldn't move. He repeated, "Louse, louse," and then his body began to shake while he slumped down to the floor. His ankle hurt, and he felt bruised and miserable. Sally yanked him to his feet.

"Lisa is hitting John, not you, Jordi. John, John. John is John. Jordi is Jordi."

"My foot—my foot," Jordi wept.

"Jordi, *your* foot. The foot of Jordi—you—Jordi. Your foot is fine.

"John—John over there with Lisa—his foot hurts—not your foot. John's foot. Jordi is Jordi. John is John."

"Jordi is Jordi—Jordi is Jordi. I'm Jordi."

Jordi felt his ankle, then his shirt. He looked at John and Lisa. Lisa's teacher—John—talked to her in a low voice. He heard the word "crayon" repeated.

"I'm Jordi—my ankle is fine. Sally, I'm me—Sally, I'm me. John is the louse. Lisa says John is the louse."

"Yes, Jordi, yes. Lisa means John, not you."

"What is a louse, Sally?"

The bus wound its way through a narrow residential street and then made a right turn on Ocean Avenue. It rattled along pleasantly—its age in quaint contrast to the modern surroundings in which it found itself. Both sides of the broad avenue were lined with tall concrete and brick buildings. Here and there a one-family house interposed itself among the massive structures.

The small houses and the bus were from an age gone by, a safer, slower time—not as efficient or comfortable perhaps, but not as slick, cold, and imposing either.

Jordi was aware of it all, even though he formulated none of it in words. He was simply aware of his feeling that the bus was warm and homelike—as were the little houses. The tall buildings intrigued him, reaching for the clouds as they did, but the mass of them, connected to one another on both sides of the street, formed a frightening gauntlet for the little bus to run through.

He looked through the back window and shivered happily. His mind's eye viewed a terrible scene indeed. From both sides buildings were crashing down to fill and obliterate Ocean Avenue. Only the bus and the occasional small houses remained intact.

The small bus miraculously escaped the ever-encroaching wave of destruction left in its wake. Huge pieces of buildings—bricks, glass, and cement boulders—smashed against the back of it. They were reduced to small particles and dust clouds. The bus was simply impervious to the explosive crashing destruction going on behind it.

Jordi looked out. Ocean Avenue was a chaotic sea of rubble. People in all states of disfigurement were unsuccessfully attempting to escape. The other cars and trucks were crushed and twisted out of shape. Their occupants screamed to no avail. But Jordi's bus joggled along unmolested and unruffled. The children in it, especially Jordi, remained warm and safe.

Jordi snuggled even deeper into his seat and smiled happily.

□ □

The classroom was light and bright.

He watched the drops of rain zigzag down the glass panes. They gathered in the corner of the window, and then the crucial drop splattered the pool in all directions. The water running down the glass fascinated him. He looked through the clear streaks left by the rain drops, and then the thought screamed out—rain forest, rain trees! He could see them too—trees raining down—getting closer to the windows. He remembered stomping the garbage can—and then the feeling welled up in him. He smashed the glass with his fists.

Twenty-eight

Within seconds he broke the three windows in the room. He was striking out, fighting the trees now. He felt so good that he didn't notice the blood gushing from his hands. He screamed in triumph. The trees were receding —and then they were no more.

Sally just caught him as he passed out.

As he came out of the haze, he heard the doctor reassuring Sally. "There were a lot of nasty cuts—but no cut tendons, nerves, or anything important. Quite a lot of blood lost, but he'll be OK. Keep the bandages on, and we'll remove the sutures in about a week."

□ □

He went to school each morning and returned in the late afternoon. This went on week after week, month after month. He was not aware of the passage of time. Nor was he aware of the change taking place in him. It wasn't a big change, and yet in a way it was. Because he was becoming more comfortable. There were fewer terrors, fewer voices, less hiding in himself. There was so much going on outside of him—so much going on between him and the world, the world and its objects—the world that used to be an emptiness, a nothingness, a hole full of potential disaster. But only he knew of this new world-relating, and even he didn't "know" it. But he felt it—yes, he felt it. And yet it hardly showed. For, after all, as the months went by, there they were, as before—Sally and Jordi, Jordi and Sally—with only a few words between them now and

Twenty-nine

then. But the words were increasing, and they were becoming more and more important as steppingstones between two people.

He called the week end the "different days." One Sunday when the streets, lacking their normal week day hustle and bustle, seemed empty, he had a thought, desert, desert—the big Sahara desert he had seen in the book. Then he thought, desert days, desert days.

But then Monday would roll around, and "Sally days" would be there again—and he would feel full and be somebody.

And so the time passed.

"Yi, yi! Yi, yi! I'll break them all, all, all. I'll break them all."

He put his heavy mittened fist through one after another of the windows.

"Jordi," she yelled. "Jordi! Stop, stop!"

She caught him and pinned his arms tightly against his body.

"What happened? Why did you break them? Don't you know, Jordi? Why?"

"I'm not Jordi. Leave me alone—I'm not Jordi. I'm me, but me isn't Jordi—not, not today, not today."

"I'm Sally today."

"Yes, you're still Sally—but me, I'm not Jordi, not today, not now."

"What's making you so angry?"

Thirty

"This place is like an ice house, like an ice house today. I'm keeping my coat on. I won't take it off."

"Keep it on if you like, but that coat is Jordi's coat, and you said you're not Jordi, so why wear his coat?"

He ran over to the rack, tore his coat off, and jumped up and down on it.

"This is my coat, this one," he said, snatching the blue tweed overcoat off the hook.

"That isn't your coat. That belongs to Robert."

"It is Robert's coat, and today it is mine."

"How come it's yours today, Jordi?"

He didn't answer.

"Will it be yours tomorrow?"

"I don't know, I don't know. If I'm jordi tomorrow, then it won't be, but I don't know."

"Oh, I see. Then you must be Robert today."

"Yes, I'm him—I mean I'm me—but me is Robert."

"How come you are Robert?"

"I don't know. I just am Robert, that's all."

"How did you become him?"

He didn't answer.

"All right, Robert," she said. "When did you become him?"

He still ignored her.

"I thought you were Jordi when you left here yesterday."

"I was," he said. "I was—but he took Jordi away from me. He took him away."

"He?"

"Yes, he, Robert."

"Well, how did he, Robert, do that?"

"On my bus, on my school bus, that's how."

"On the bus?"

"He took my seat, he took it from me. He made me sit in his. I had to sit in his. I said, 'Give me my seat, give me my Jordi seat,' but they laughed."

"Who, Jordi?"

He ignored her.

"I mean who laughed?"

He still didn't answer.

"I mean who laughed, Robert?"

"Now I understand you, now I do. It was the train man. The train man, he laughed at me and said, 'Take Robert's seat. All the seats are the same. We can't waste time. Come on, kid, take Robert's seat!'"

"Well, where is Jordi now?" she asked.

"Over there," he said, pointing to Robert. "Over there, that's the Jordi boy, the one that sat in the Jordi seat."

Sally walked over to the coat rack and took down John's big brown coat. It was much too large for her. It came down to her ankles, and the sleeves flapped below her hands.

"I guess I've got the wrong coat on," she said, flapping the sleeves up and down.

"Yes, Sally, that coat isn't yours. That's John's coat—Lisa's teacher, John."

"Then who am I? If I'm wearing John's coat, who am I?"

"Oh, come on, you're silly."

"I'm silly. I guess I am silly with this great big coat on."

"I mean Sally—Sally silly, silly Sally."

"Yes, Jordi, I'm Sally. Maybe silly, but still Sally, and, no matter whose coat I put on, I am still Sally."

She went back to the rack and put one coat on after another. Each time she put another coat on, she asked,

"Who am I?" And each time he repeated, "You're Sally, I know you're Sally."

Then she took his hand and said, "Let's go up to William's office." When she got to the director's office, she asked him if he could leave for a few minutes. He said, "Hi, Jordi," as he closed the door behind him. Then Sally sat down in William's chair.

"Whose chair is this?"

"William's chair."

"Where is William?"

"William just went out."

"So who am I?"

"You, you're Sally—silly Sally," he grinned.

She got up. "Sit here, in William's chair." He sat down.

"Where is William?" she asked.

"Oh, he's still outside, Sally. You know that."

"Well, where are you sitting?"

"I'm sitting in the big chair."

"Whose chair?"

"The William chair."

"And who are you?"

He looked into her eyes very solemnly. Then his face crinkled into a big grin, and he said, "I'm Jordi. Yes, Sally, I'm truly Jordi."

□ □

"You know, Sally—the trees are gone."

"What trees, Jordi?"

"The rain trees."

"Oh? Tell me about them."

"The trees that rain down—the trees from the rain forest. You saw them yesterday when I beat them off. The day I got my hands sewed up."

"That wasn't yesterday. That was a year ago, Jordi—a year ago. Remember the calendar we studied, Jordi? Remember the days, the weeks, the months—years?"

"I remember. Yes, I do, Sally."

"Yesterday is just a day ago—the day before today, the day before you got up this morning. You hurt your hands many days ago—a year ago."

"Yes, Sally, I understand. It wasn't yesterday; it was twelve months ago.

"But, Sally, let's talk. I know about days, but the trees—I want to talk about them."

"I'm sorry, Jordi. Go ahead, tell me about the trees."

"Well, the trees—when it rains now, just rain drops come down, not like before Sally."

"Before?"

"You remember rain forest, rain trees—coming down to look for me. They were so scary, so scary," he said, trembling.

"You must have been angry, Jordi. You must have been scared of being angry."

"Angry, me angry. But the trees looked angry."

"Jordi, do you know what a rain forest is? Come, let's look it up in the encyclopedia."

She read the big book out loud. She read all about equatorial rain forests and rain trees and explained the material to him in detail. She ended by saying, "So, you see, Jordi, rain forest doesn't mean trees or forests raining down."

Thirty-four

Jordi was fascinated. "Sally, does it say all that in the book?"

"Yes, Jordi, it's all here in this encyclopedia."

"Encyclopedia." He repeated the word several times.

"Would you like to be able to read this book, Jordi?"

"Could I, Sally?"

"Well, you can learn to read, Jordi, if you like."

"Could I, Sally, could I?"

"Yes, Jordi."

"Toosies, toosies—hop, skip, and jump." Then she lost interest and walked over to him.

"Hi, kid, wanna play?"

He said, "Play, play, go away."

"Hey, you're funny, sonny."

She took his hand and pulled him along. But he yanked his hand away.

He thought, she will leave me.

He ran to the corner and stood perfectly still. Maybe now she wouldn't notice him, but she ran after him and once again took his hand.

"C'mon, kid, let's play. . . . What's your name? Me, I'm Muriel. Who are you? What does your mommy call you?"

"Jordi."

"Georgie, porgie, puddin' and pie, kiss the girls and made them cry.

"Kiss, piss, fiss. Georgie, porgie."

Thirty-five

He screwed up his face. "Georgie, Georgie—who is Georgie?"

"You silly dilly—you—you're Georgie. . . . Dilly, dilly—Willie, Willie? You're funny, honey. Honey, bunny—money—yummy.

"Let's play, Georgie—let's play. Muriel will show you. You're yummy—yum yum, Georgie."

"Jordi," he screamed. "Jordi—I'm Jordi. Tell—Sally, tell—me, I'm Jordi."

"Oh, Jordi. Lordy Jordi—no more porgie Georgie.

"Well, I'm Lisa—Lisa, not Muriel. Like the cigar Daddy smokes—Muriel.

"What's that you're jiggling, Jordi?"

"Jiggling?" He laughed. "I'm jiggling my jiggler. Jiggle, jiggle—wiggle, wiggle—my friend, my friend—my jiggler."

"Make me a jiggler, Jordi—would you, huh?"

"Sally? Where are you, Sally?"

"Here, Jordi, right here. Come, Jordi, Lisa, let's go to lunch."

□ □

"Promise, Sally, promise we'll take a train ride all over the old stations. I'll show them all to you, Sally—the IRT, the BMT. Will you come with me, Sally—will you?"

"Of course, Jordi. It sounds so nice."

"When, Sally, when?"

"Now, if you like—yes, right now."

"Will we pass the water tower on the way to the station?"

"Yes, we will go down by way of the tower. But first finish lunch, Jordi."

"Why, Sally?"

"Aren't you hungry, Jordi?"

"No."

"But if you eat, you'll grow big and strong."

Jordi dashed from the table, ran upstairs, and grabbed the yardstick. He broke half a dozen windows before Sally caught up with him.

"Why, Jordi? Why?"

He didn't answer.

Sally held him closer. He yanked himself out of her arms and ran out of the room. Sally followed.

She sat with him the entire afternoon. Not a word passed between them that day, the next, and the next—not for three weeks. They just walked around together. Jordi knew she was there, but his feeling of emptiness just cut him off from her and everything else.

Then he felt like taking a train ride, and he thought of Sally, and he forgot to be silent.

"Sally, can we take the train today?"

"Yes. We can, and we shall."

After lunch they walked about eight blocks to the water tower.

"It's a lovely tower, Sally."

"How is it lovely, Jordi?"

"It's high and it's quiet and it's alone."

"You like it, Jordi?"

"I like it."

"How much, a little or a lot?" Sally asked, demonstrating with her hands.

"Much, much—this much and more, Sally—much more. A lot—a big lot."

"I guess you love the tower, Jordi."

He felt the good bursting feeling well up in his chest.

"I love the tower. I do love the water tower."

"Wonderful, Jordi, wonderful. Now you know what love feels like."

"Love. I feel love—I feel love, Sally?"

His face glowed, the feeling spread through him, and he felt warm and nice and comfortable. And then the feeling evaporated and in its place left a scare. He took Sally's hand and said, "Let's take the train now."

On the train he drew his eyes away from the tunnel and his ever-arriving, wonderful stations. He faced her.

"Sally, yesterday I didn't like you, not even a little much."

"You mean you disliked me, Jordi?"

"I did, I did dislike you."

"How did I hurt you yesterday, Jordi?"

"Sally, I want to be little. I want to be a boy." Then the words exploded forth: "You said I'd be big and strong."

"Oh," she said, "three weeks ago, yesterday."

"Yes, Sally. If I'm big, I won't be a boy any more. I don't want to be big, Sally—just a boy, just Jordi."

"You must have been very angry with me."

"Yes, Sally, yes. Let me be little—let me be me, just Jordi."

"Jordi, you will always be you—and some day you will understand this better."

"I like you now, Sally."

Thirty-eight

"I like you too, Jordi. But if you don't like me—if sometimes you dislike me or dislike me much, hate me—that's all right too."

But he had lost interest and was watching the stations again.

□ □

The monkey bars, crisscrossing up and down, forward and backward, intrigued him. There was no question that his jiggler pointed in their direction. But what if he got caught in the middle of all that iron? What if he couldn't get out?

He walked over cautiously and touched the closest bar. It was cold. A sinister chill ran through him. But the jiggler pointed in that direction again. This time he touched a bar warmed by the sun. This felt different, more inviting, but he was still afraid. It looked like a wonderful toy to climb over and swing from. And it looked like an awful monster that could tangle you up, crush you, and kill you.

He couldn't move from the spot. He wanted to run toward and away from it at the same time. Indecision paralyzed him. His face was flushed, and he ground his teeth. Tears streamed down his cheeks, but his legs remained planted.

Her low voice, soft and smooth, said, "Try it. It's fun, Jordi—fun—a toy. I'll show you."

She swung from a high bar, bringing her legs out perpendicular to her body. Then from the top of them she yelled, "Yo-ho, Jordi! It's nice up here."

His legs kicked out of their invisible trap. "Wait for me, Sally. I'm coming to look at the sky too."

On the way back to school he said, "I was afraid it would tangle me."

"Oh?"

"The cold ones. The warm ones were nicer."

Sally told him how the sun warmed some of the bars. She then told him that he could tangle himself but could not get tangled by it—or by anything else that wasn't alive.

Before he went to sleep that night he thought about it a lot and he began to get the feeling of the difference between living and nonliving objects. By the next day some of the magic of the monkey bars was gone—but so was the monster.

They went back the next day. He looked at them but suddenly realized how thin the bars were. Maybe they couldn't hold him. What if he fell through them? They were so shiny. He could feel the whole structure crashing down on him.

"Let's go back, Sally."

"Why?"

"I'm afraid. Please, Sally—please."

"Let's play on the bars for a while first."

"No."

"They can't hurt you, Jordi."

"But if they fall, Sally."

"They are made of iron—very strong stuff, Jordi. They can hold twenty of us."

"But not me, Sally—not me."

"Oh, Jordi, so you're not afraid of the bars being weak?"

"I am afraid."

"You're afraid that you won't hold yourself up, Jordi.

But you're strong. Look at your arms and legs—how sturdy they are."

"I'm strong like the iron, Sally?"

"Well, not like the iron—but good and strong. Strong enough, Jordi, so that you can hold yourself on the bars. That is, if you don't want to fall, Jordi."

"No, no, I don't want to fall."

"Then you won't fall, Jordi. Let's go."

They played on the bars, and it was fun. He felt strong swinging up and back. He smiled at her as they looked at the blue sky.

"Fun, Jordi?"

"Yes—and I'm strong, Sally. Me—Jordi—I'm strong."

He even forgot to take his jiggler out on the way home from school.

□ □

Several months later he sat at his mother's sewing table.

He looked at the crayons and took out all the short pieces. That left him seven long ones. He couldn't make up his mind. First he started with orange, then red, then black. He finally started to fill the fish in with purple.

But the point was worn down. He tried awfully hard but couldn't stay within the lines. He held his hand stiff and tried not to bend his wrist, but this only made it worse. Tears streamed down his cheeks, and he could hardly see. He held his right hand with his left, but to no avail. Grief and hopelessness flooded him. He heard himself thinking, can't, can't, can't—Jordi can't. Jordi can't. No good, no good, no good.

There was little of the fish left now. The purple made wilder and wilder streaks all over the paper. This time there was no hesitancy in his choice. He took the red crayon. Holding it like a knife, he stabbed the paper again and again. Then he took the black and blotted out the remains of the fish altogether. He took the sharp pencil and stabbed and tore and stabbed and tore over and over again.

The paper was in shreds now. His sobbing tore out of him in spasms. It was interrupted only by short gasps of breath. His body twisted to and fro, and his shoulders heaved up and down. He felt himself drowning in anguish.

Through his tears he suddenly saw the tattered paper. It was monstrous. This torn-up red, purple, black, stabbed, blotted-out fish was horror itself. He screamed and ran. He could feel the thing chasing him. This bleeding, stumpy thing he had wounded. This monster he had manufactured.

The form and color of it kaleidoscoped. He pictured it short, round, fat, tall, black, purple, sharp, dull with jagged holes and hating him. He stopped. He hit his jaw with his closed fist. He hit himself again and again.

His face was very swollen, but the monster had gone. Only a piece of colored paper remained. He crumpled it into a ball and dropped it into the basket.

He heard the key in the door, and then she came in. He heard her say, "Oh, God, oh, God. My God. Why, why? Your face, your face, my baby, my baby. Why, why did you do it, why?"

He let himself be led into the bathroom, and the cold compress felt good. He heard her sobbing but couldn't understand why.

Forty-two

"But, Mama, I feel good. I do, I do feel good."

"Why did you beat yourself? Why, Jordi, why?"

"It was the fish monster. I had to get it away—I just had to. It was—oh, Mama, I don't want to hit myself. I don't want to. I don't know, I don't know—how—how. Oh, Mama, help me," he cried, and then she stopped crying.

He felt himself held by her and felt his bruised cheek being kissed. He snuggled into her arms. Then she led him into the living room and gave him the chocolate bar she had in her bag. He stopped crying, ate it, and felt better.

"I like you. Mom, I like you."

"I love you, Jordi. I love you very much."

"How much, Mom? How much?"

"A great big bunch and then some—more than anything, more than anything in this whole world."

"Gee, I feel nice, Mom. It feels good in here." He pointed to his chest. "It feels warm and good in here."

"I'm glad. I'm so glad, Jordi."

He went outside and walked to the water tower. He sat and stared at it for a while. Then he walked around it and looked at it some more. After a while he started to walk home. He made sure his jiggler was in his pocket but didn't take it out. Just knowing he had it with him made him feel safer.

On the way home he thought about Sally and wondered what words they would rhyme in school. Then he thought of the word "rhyme," and then "slime" and "climb." He pictured himself climbing the water tower. On top of it he would be away and higher than anyone else. But he would have to come down to see Sally and her and him too. Then he thought, her and him, Mama and Papa.

When they ate supper, his jaw ached, and he thought about it.

"Do you feel all right?" his father asked.

"Yes, yes."

"But your jaw, Jordi, does it hurt?"

"My jaw—yes, it hurts. It does hurt."

"I'm sorry it hurts, Jordi."

"Me, I'm sorry too. I'm sorry my jaw hurts."

He rubbed it a little too hard and winced.

After supper he was very tired. He lay on his bed thinking about things for a while. In a very short time he fell asleep.

He dreamed that he was walking on the kitchen floor. He walked up and back, swinging his jiggler to and fro. Suddenly he realized that the floor had a big fish outlined on it, and nearby lay a great big purple crayon. He took the crayon and started to color the fish. But then the crayon turned into a Pogo stick. Jordi rode the Pogo— jumping from spot to spot and depositing purple wherever he landed. Soon the whole fish was purple—and there wasn't a spot outside of the lines.

Then a funny thing happened. The fish rose up from the floor and became a real live purple fish. Then it said, "I like you Jordi. You made me a nice color, and I'll always be your friend."

Then he tied a long string all around the fish and led him through the deserted street like a dog on a leash. And people woke up and began to fill the streets. He wasn't afraid, though, because he had his fish friend with him, who was bigger even then a big dog.

He got up the next morning feeling that there was more to him. He felt as though there was more of him than his usual self—sort of like a piece had been added. He looked in the dresser mirror and felt disappointed that there was no addition to himself. His dimensions were all the same. He was no heavier and no taller.

But the feeling stuck with him. There was just more of him, even if he couldn't see it. Maybe there was more inside him—inside, where he couldn't see but sometimes felt different things.

The feeling made him walk differently. His feet moved more importantly; his steps were surer. Everything about himself felt more solid. When he got on the bus that morning, he almost felt it creak down in response to his added something. He remembered nothing of his dream. It was as if it never happened.

When he got to school, he and Sally rhymed words for a while and then sat down at the long low table.

"I feel funny, Sally."

"Oh?"

"Sort of like more."

"Like more, Jordi?"

"More—draw, draw. Let's draw, Sally."

She took down a big box of crayons and paper.

For a while he just drew lines—then broader lines, and then boxes and circles here and there. Then he drew a series of dots from one corner of the page to the other. Then he drew lines connecting the dots.

"Sally, could we fill in something?"

"Sure. What would you like to fill in, Jordi?"

He didn't answer.

"Here. Here is a triangle, Jordi."

"A triangle?" he asked.

"Yes." She explained how a triangle consisted of three sides and three angles—one between each pair of sides.

Then she drew a circle and a rectangle and defined and explained each of them to him.

Jordi was intrigued with what he heard. Listening to her was great fun.

"Gee, I like this, Sally. I like to play this way."

"Me too," she said.

Then he took a purple crayon and started to fill in the large triangle—the one he now knew was an equilateral triangle. He was very careful, but, unwittingly, he moved just outside the lower left angle.

"Oh, oh," he moaned, "Sally, I feel funny. Oh."

"What's wrong, Jordi? What? Tell me."

He hit himself with his closed fist again and again.

"Hold my hand, Sally. Help me—hold me."

She held his hands between hers as he moaned, "Oh, oh." Then she managed to get him on her lap. She bent over him, held her arms around him, and hugged him tightly.

He felt warm and safe.

After a while he stopped moaning. But she continued to hold him. Soon she started to hum and sing to him—and after a few minutes he hummed along with her. They sat humming and singing for more than an hour. Then they walked around the room and looked at all the new pictures recently placed on the walls.

They had meat loaf, potatoes, and green peas for lunch. Jordi attacked it with relish and even ate some more potatoes before he gulped down his Jell-O.

When they were back upstairs—sitting at the table—Sally started to talk.

"Why were you angry at yourself, Jordi?"

"Angry?"

"Yes—before lunch when you hit yourself and asked me to hold your hands?"

"Oh—I was angry?" he asked with some wonderment. Then he answered himself. "Yes, I was. I went outside the line." Tears started to fill his eyes. "I went outside the line. I couldn't help it—I just couldn't."

"The line, Jordi?"

"Yes, when I filled in with the crayon."

"I see."

"Do you, Sally?"

"Yes. I understand. But, Jordi, you don't have to draw perfectly. It's all right to go outside the line. I'll love you anyway.

"Jordi, you draw just for fun. If it has to be perfect, it's no fun."

"Perfect?" he questioned.

"Yes—you know—just so, all within the line—exactly so. Nothing—nothing is perfect."

"But, Sally, if it's outside the line the triangle won't be a triangle anymore. It will be all over. It will be like wild—like a panther."

"But, Jordi, even if it isn't a triangle anymore, it's OK. And a little bit won't matter anyway. It will still be a triangle. And anyway, Jordi, a drawing isn't a living thing. But, regardless of how you draw, Jordi, you will still be you, and I'll love you inside or outside the line."

"A drawing isn't a living thing," he repeated. "A drawing isn't a living thing.

"Draw an empty fish—draw a fish, Sally."

She outlined a big fish on a large white sheet of paper.

He filled it in with purple. Then he looked at her—and scribbled the crayon outside the outline. He looked at her again. And they both started to laugh together. And they laughed and laughed until their bellies hurt. Then she hugged him and hugged him and kissed his cheek. And it didn't feel bruised at all.

After several months Jordi had learned a considerable amount about addition, subtraction, and the multiplication tables and some facts about division.

One day he asked if they could talk more about the angles—triangles and rectangles. Sally told him all about degrees in angles. Then she went on and explained about circles and area and volume. Jordi was very attentive and absorbed it readily. But then Sally explained that this would be discussed later on in high school and college. She described high school and college and working. Jordi listened but wasn't too interested. Later on they resumed their reading work, and he liked the way she looked when he read a whole page from the reader without stopping.

Just before he went home that day he turned to her and said, "Sally, you really became a teacher in this room."

□ □

He got off the bus.

"Hello, Sally."

"Hi, Jordi."

"School is nice. I like it. The public, it's the public I don't like."

"The public?"

"Yes, they—the strangers. I was with strangers the whole Saturday and Sunday—the whole week end."

"But you were home, Jordi."

"Home, home with the public—with strangers."

"Your mother and father were home, Jordi."

"They were public also—they were all strangers. They were all away from me—not close like you and me now here in school, Sally."

"All? Who else was there?"

"The funny baby and Tillie and Joseph."

"Funny baby?"

"Billy—Cousin Billy. He's a little bitty baby."

"But you said he was funny, Jordi."

"Well—he was crying—they couldn't make him stop. They all jumped around the room—and Billy made such funny faces. I laughed. They made mean faces at me. I laughed some more—his face was so funny. They tried to make me stop. Then one of the public—she hit me."

"She? Your mother?"

"Yes—but this week end she was no mother. She was a stranger."

"You mean because she didn't understand you—she was strange."

"Yes—but you understand me, Sally."

"Not always. Sometimes it takes time. And sometimes it takes the people at home time."

"Like sometimes I can't understand them?"

"That's right, Jordi."

"Let's rhyme words, Sally."

"OK."

They sat down at the table.

"Cat," she began.

"Bat."
"Fat."
"Sat."
It was soon time for lunch.

□ □

He looked at the ceiling and thought of the sky, the earth, the street, and the subway station. He remembered somebody saying that the world was round. He pictured a round globe hanging in mid-air and then thought of everybody walking to and fro on the big ball. Then he pictured a staircase going down into the ball and coming to a bright station. He saw a train run through the globe and stop at the station. A sandy-haired little boy got on the train holding a string attached to a doorknob between his right thumb and forefinger. The train left the station and rode all around the inside of the globe. The boy walked from one car to the next and finally came to the first one. He hung the doorknob out the front window.

Then the train followed the jiggler—zig, zag, this way and that. Yes, he was using the magic string knob to lead the train all over the inside of the earth. It was actually working. The magic jiggler was controlling the train.

Then he realized that the boy was getting larger. He had the same face and the same sandy hair, but he was big now—very big. Soon he was a giant and almost filled the whole car. He could tell that the boy giant was afraid of nothing. There he was with his jiggler and his train going wherever he liked. Nobody could stop him. The earth was his.

Then Jordi saw the boy wave the jiggler around outside the front window. And the train left the track, and there was no track in front of it or anywhere in sight. But the train went faster than ever—whiz, whiz, whiz. It cut through the earth. It was cutting the globe up like a big piece of cake, only it was doing it from the inside. And then he saw big pieces of the globe caving in all over the train. But the giant boy and his jiggler led the train right through it all to slice up the earth some more—and more and more.

When he looked at the top of the earth, people were running all over the place, but they couldn't get away. They were being buried by the big cave-ins. Buildings were crumbling all over. It was dark, but the sky was bright blood red. And in the light of the redness Jordi could see the earth and many things on it falling down, down and crumbling all up. The giant had a big smile on his face now.

The earth, and everything on it, was gone. Only the train remained, and the giant boy and his jiggler led it from station to lighted station through space.

Jordi rolled over and fell asleep at once.

□ □

The bath felt very nice. It was warm, and he was alone. He pushed the piece of wood around the tub and watched it skim over his knees and then back again over his belly. Then he held it down on the bottom of the tub and let it go suddenly, watching it shoot to the surface. He let the wood float and then dropped the bar of soap on it from different heights. Splash, splash, but the wood popped right up again. Then he thought of his penis. First he squeezed it; then he rubbed it up and down. It felt nice, and it was good to be alone. When his penis stood up, he stared at it a while and wondered how this magic took place. There it was again much bigger than before and standing straight up. He thought, first it's like the jiggler, then it's like the water tower.

After a while he got up and soaped himself all over. Then sat down and let the water get real cloudy and soapy.

He lay on his back, and almost his whole body was hidden by the cloudy water. He pushed his foot through. He could see it but not the rest of his leg. He suddenly felt that his foot was detached from his leg and the rest of his body. He became very frightened and lifted his foot quickly, and there it was, still part of the rest of him. He felt much better but didn't dare lift his foot that way again—at least not in the cloudy water.

He played with the wooden boat some more. It glided over his belly. Then he let the dirty water out of the tub and let in new clean clear water.

Then he felt interested in his belly button. He looked at it and screwed his finger around in it. Then he noticed how a little water remained in his belly button each time he brought his belly up out of the water.

He had a funny thought: Button is to close up something. Belly button closes the belly. What if it opened up and a little water got in?

He could already see himself swelling, swelling, swelling and then—pop—exploding.

And yet he knew with his thoughts, that it wouldn't happen. He knew that his belly button wouldn't open, and he even doubted that it had anything to do with his insides anyway. But the feeling about it and the picture of water leaking in persisted. So he felt a little silly but got up and dried himself. He made sure no water remained in his belly button.

He sat with them and stared at his father. He waited for him to talk. He liked to hear his voice. It was soft and deep and made him feel warm. The thunder was the same way too. His mother's voice was high and thinner. Sometimes it stuck and cut, but sometimes it was high and bright like lightning.

"Jordi, would you like to go to the zoo?"

"Yes."

And then they left the house. He held his hand and let himself be led even though he knew the train route they were taking.

When they got off at the station, they had a long block to walk to the zoo. He kicked a can he found all along the way. Then they saw the elephants, monkeys, and lions.

His father knew that the panthers pleased him most, so they stayed at the cage for a long time.

Jordi watched the animal pace up and down and wondered what would happen if it got loose. He liked its shininess and the rippling way it moved. Woosh, woosh—he could see it tear through the crowd and everybody running in all directions. Everybody but me, he thought as he took his jiggler out and dangled it.

His father bought some popcorn and peanuts. They sat on the bench and fed themselves and the squirrels. The squirrels pleased him very much, taking the nuts from his fingers the way they did.

□ □

"Boy, is he angry! Jesus Christ, he is *mad!* Boy! Look at him—just look, Sally."

He had the magazine open to an insurance ad. There was a picture of a train wreck and a man looking at it with a startled, worried expression on his face.

"Wow! This man is *angry*. Wow, is he angry—an angry man, a truly angry man."

Jordi walked up and down the room. He was too excited to do anything else that day. He felt this man's feeling. And seeing a man whose feeling was his feeling in a big magazine was very exciting. He was so excited he hardly ate lunch that day. He carried the magazine with him wherever he went for a whole week. Then he asked Sally if they could hang the magazine on the bulletin board. They tried tacking it up but finally settled on just putting up the page with the picture.

He walked up to the wall again and again. Then, almost a month after they put the picture up, he left Sally at the low table and walked over to Lisa and John. He stood close to them and watched Lisa make the Indian bead ring.

"Hi, kid—hi," she said.

"Hello, hello. Come with me, Lisa. I want to show you." She looked to John.

"Go, Lisa," he said. "Go with Jordi."

"All right, Jordi Pordi. Let's amble, let's scramble, and let's go—but slow—ho, ho."

He led her to the picture on the wall. He pointed to it. "Jesus Christ, is he angry! Boy, he is! He is—he is sure truly angry."

"Jordi, Pordi, let's play jacks. OK? Jacks, facts—let's go, Jo."

"But, Lisa, the man—look, look at him—how he looks. Boy, is he mad! He is *sore!*"

"Sore, tore—what for?" She ran back to John.

He looked at the picture again, shrugged his shoulders, and went back to Sally at the table.

"That Lisa–Muriel kid is funny. Angry—angry—she doesn't know what it is—angry. Funny, honey—that girl is funny. She sure is."

"Well, we're not all the same, Jordi."

"But angry—Sally, I told her about angry—and she walked away."

"About anger, Jordi," she corrected.

"Yes, Sally—about anger."

He went on. "She is funny, that kid. She is funny."

"Well, we all have problems, Jordi."

"Problems. Gee, that's a funny way to say it—problems. What do you mean—problems?"

"Well, like you, Jordi—when you were afraid of the monkey bars."

"Yes, Sally—and like the garbage cans and the rain trees."

"That's right, Jordi."

"But, Sally, that was the old Jordi.

"Do you remember, do you remember the old Jordi, Sally? Do you remember him? He couldn't ride a bike. He was afraid of the cans. Sometimes he was afraid to talk. He had problems. He had lots of problems, Sally—boy, oh boy, he truly had problems.

"But now, Sally, now the new Jordi is here. He can walk and ride and talk and go on the monkey bars. He can get angry and he can say 'gee whizz,' and he can draw outside the line.

"And, Sally, the new Jordi—me—I know about triangles and I can read too."

"You sure can, Jordi—and how you can."

Lisa walked by. She was talking to herself.

"Muriel is my name—and it's the same, the same."

Jordi looked at Sally and then asked, "Is her problem showing, Sally? Is Lisa's problem showing?"

"Yes, I guess it is, Jordi. You could say that. Her problem is showing."

"Sally, it's a long time, a long time. Isn't it, Sally?"

"A long time what is? What, Jordi? What is a long time?"

"You, Sally. You—you and me. Is it years? Is it years and years, Sally?"

"Jordi, it's years—but it seems longer to me too."

"Sally, it's like you were always. Like when I think of it —it's like it was black before."

"Black, Jordi?"

"Last night I thought of before. It seemed so long ago,

like it wasn't. Then I knew it was—and when I thought of it—I saw it like a darkness. It was all black—I got scared. I jumped out of bed—and put the light on. Then I felt better. Then I thought, Sally, and the blackness became gone. I said 'Sally,' then I turned off the light—and it was dark—but it was light."

□ □

Several months passed.

After he had come home one afternoon, he went into the bathroom, locked the door, and then took out his penis and examined it. He thought it looked like a toadstool he once saw in a picture book. He rubbed it a while and before long felt better—after it got soft he looked at it again before he put it back, and it seemed longer to him. Then he looked in the mirror and saw that he had got bigger than he had remembered himself. Then he buttoned his trousers and went outside.

He began to walk to the water tower but saw the skinny boy playing stoop ball several houses down. He walked over to the ball player and watched. He thought, how skinny he is. But he was awed at his ability to throw the ball. He really hit the steps hard, and he caught it each time too. Jordi forgot about the water tower and just stood there with his hands at his sides, watching. After a while "Skinny"—Jordi now thought of him by that name—stopped playing, put the ball in his pocket, and walked off. He went back to his house.

"Mom, I want a ball."

"A ball, Jordi? Sure. What kind?"

"Kind?" he asked.

"Yes. A little one, a big one? A football?"

"Just a little one, Mom. A hand ball—not for feet, but for playing with hands."

"All right, dear, here's a quarter. The man at the candy store will give you a ball for it."

He went to the candy store with the coin clenched tightly in his fist. Then he went inside. It was kind of dark and smelled sour. The fat man with the red face walked toward him and began to ask what he wanted. Jordi turned around and quickly walked out.

Then he walked to the water tower, still holding the quarter tightly clenched in his fist. He stared at the tower a while and then went home.

"Did you buy the ball, Jordi?"

"No."

"Do you still have the quarter?"

"Yes. I'll buy it tomorrow, Mom. I'll buy it with Sally."

That night before he went to bed he stood in front of his dresser mirror wearing only his shorts. Then he examined himself. He thought he was taller and heavier than "Skinny." Then he sucked his stomach in, and even that way he wasn't as skinny as "Skinny." He thought of swinging on the monkey bars and being strong. He said to the mirror, "Jordi, you're a sturdy boy, a sturdy boy. Jordi, you're strong, truly strong."

He practiced throwing an imaginary ball against the mirror and catching it. Then he thought of doing it against the steps. He pictured "Skinny" watching him. Then he saw himself missing the ball and "Skinny" laughing. He suddenly felt chilled and shuddered.

He got into bed and pulled the covers up to his chin. He felt cozy and warm. The orange glow of the ceiling lights added to his warm feeling. He let it burn all night.

The next day he showed Sally the quarter and told her it was for a ball.

"I went to the store at home, but I got scared and ran out. Can we get it at the candy store near here, Sally?"

"Sure we can, Jordi. We'll go down after lunch and buy a ball. But what kind of game do you want to play with it?"

"Well—you know, Sally—like I saw this skinny boy play on my home street. He was throwing the ball against the steps and catching it. Boy, he could do it strong. He is skinny but strong."

"That's called stoop ball," she said.

Sally went on and described the game to him. Then she described baseball, football, and basketball. She got the basketball from the basement and showed it to him. He held the ball, and his hands felt nice rubbing around it. She asked if he would like to shoot for baskets in the schoolyard, but he said, "No, I just want to buy a little white ball and play Skinny's game, stoop ball."

" 'Buy,' Jordi? You said 'buy.' "

"Yes, like my mother buys in the store."

"Good. Let's spend the rest of the time before lunch talking about buying and money."

Then they talked about the different kinds of stores and things to buy. They talked all about pennies, nickels, dimes, and quarters. Sally demonstrated them all to him, including paper money. Then they pretended to buy things from each other.

Jordi thought Sally seemed very excited and happy, and he felt good too. She went upstairs and got a lot of coins and bills from William. Then they made the big room into different kinds of stores. They sold each other everything in the room, and they made change and bought up everything and sold it back.

After lunch Jordi wanted to play with the money some more before going out to buy the ball.

This time Sally tried to give him a better idea about the relative value and prices of things. Jordi caught on very quickly and had a lot of fun guessing the price of eggs, butter, a lunch, a chair, a car, and many other things.

Sally then went on to explain how people earned money and how stores made profits by buying low and selling high. Jordi asked her about checks, but when she started to explain about them, he finally lost interest and asked her if they could buy the ball now.

On the way to the store Sally explained more about how either one hundred or one hundred fifty wins in stoop ball. Then she casually asked him, "Who is that boy 'Skinny' you mentioned?"

But his mind was elsewhere.

"Sally, you know the subway tokens are like money."

"Yes, indeed, Jordi. They're worth fifteen cents each."

"Sally, I used to take them off the dresser and sometimes I just walked under the turning thing without one."

"How did you know about the tokens, Jordi?"

"Pop, he used them when we went to the zoo. He let me put it in the thing too."

"In the slot," she added.

"Yes, in the slot. Then he used to put them on the dresser. So, one day I took one and tried it, and went to some stations."

They both walked into the candy store. Jordi held his quarter out and went over to the woman behind the counter.

"Here is a quarter, twenty-five pennies. This is for you —and for me, I want a ball."

He hesitated, then added, "I want to buy a ball—a little plain white one for playing stoop ball."

The woman smiled at him and said, "That's a lot of pennies. For twenty-five cents you can get a Spalding."

He looked at Sally questioningly, and she nodded, yes.

After they left the store, he asked her what "a Spalding" meant. She explained about different makes and different qualities of the same article and about the differences these made in relative money value. He listened attentively and then said, "Gee, Sally, you know a lot of a lot of a lot of things."

Then Sally stopped walking and turned him around to face her. She held his shoulders and looked into his eyes and said, "Jordi, today you talked to a stranger. You just walked into that store and talked to somebody you didn't know. Not only that, you asked for something and nothing bad happened, Jordi. It came out fine."

"I talked to a stranger," he repeated. "I talked to a stranger—you know, Sally—and then she wasn't so strange anymore."

Then they walked back to school to practice stoop ball.

It wasn't at all easy. Sally told him to be careful of cars when he went to retrieve the ball. And he did a lot of retrieving. Each time he hit a point the ball went over his head. But he learned fast, and before long he was a stoop-ball player.

After an hour his arm hurt, but he kept playing. After a while he tallied up points, and then it was even more fun. But when his arm felt real heavy, he said, "Let's rhyme words or something, Sally."

He played lots of stoop ball after that, both at school and at home. He carried the ball constantly, and on some days he was so busy holding and squeezing it that he hardly remembered his jiggler.

□ □

"I can climb the bars now, Sally."

"What was that, Jordi? I didn't hear you."

"The bars, monkey bars—now I can climb on them and play."

"Yes, you sure can."

"Sally, it's the bars and things, other things too."

"Yes, there's been much, Jordi—many things."

And there were things, many things. There was incident after incident. There were bars, many bars—bars to cross, bars to climb, bars to knock down—and they did it. And it was hard work. But they struggled, and the bars came down.

Spring had come. It was a warm day.

"How about going over to the playground, Jordi?"

"What will we do there, Sally?"

"Well, there's the monkey bars."

"No, no, Sally, let's do something else."

"Why? Are you afraid of something, Jordi?"

"No, no," he hastened to reassure her.

"It's just—well." He seemed embarrassed.

"Jordi, come on now, what's doing?" she asked.

"Well, Sally—well, the other children playing there—well, Sally—well—they're small, Sally. They're so small."

"You're right, Jordi. I hadn't realized—you are bigger than the other children. I guess I sometimes forget you're a big boy now. You're over twelve now—over twelve years old."

She seemed very pleased with it all. He couldn't understand why but kind of felt happy because she seemed to feel so good.

After lunch Sally said she wanted to read something important and would he like to busy himself for a while. He welcomed being alone and told her he would be on the stoop of the school building.

He sat there a while, and then he took out his jiggler. He noticed how hard it was to get it out of his pocket. Then he took the ball from his other pocket. He weighed and balanced them, one in each hand. Then he thought to himself, my old jiggler. He put it back in his pocket and began to play stoop ball. Then for the first time in his memory the jiggler bothered him. He felt the shaft of the doorknob dig into his thigh each time he threw the ball. He took the jiggler out again and went into the building to find Sally at her desk.

"Will you hold my jiggler for me, Sally? I want to play stoop ball."

She said, "Sure, Jordi. Here, I'll put it in my desk drawer."

He went outside and resumed his solitary game of stoop ball.

□ □

Several weeks later it was a beautiful, dry frosty day. They went to the playground, and Jordi walked around for a while, just breathing in the crispy air and feeling good.

He watched the children on the monkey bars and thought that they looked just like the little monkeys in the zoo.

Sally sat on the bench and read while he explored the entire playground. Then he saw the group of boys playing handball. They were about ten years old. There were three of them, and the very dark boy yelled out to him.

"Hey, fella, how about some handball? I need a partner."

Jordi said, "I don't know how."

"Don't worry, I'll show you. My name is Billy. What's your name?"

"I'm Jordi."

"Come on, Jordi." Billy beckoned, and Jordi joined the group.

□ □

He had no idea that four years had passed since he first entered the "ice house."

When Sally told him about the impending examination, he vaguely remembered the ink blots, the cold stethoscope, and somebody talking and bothering him.

After they talked about it a while he lost interest, and they went back to what they were doing.

□

This twelve-year-old, white, sandy-haired boy has been examined, tested, and interviewed by the psychological and psychiatric diagnostic and planning staff.

His size, weight, and appearance are not unusual. There is no evidence of physical impairment of any kind. There is no evidence of organicity. Contact is good, and attention span is fair. He hesitates at the beginning of the interview situation but soon adjusts and relates adequately.

He is well oriented in all spheres and demonstrates good memory function for both recent and past events. There is at present no evidence of secondary phenomena, hallucinations and delusions not being demonstrable. Impulse control is fair. His affective display is somewhat shallower than normal but is appropriate for the most part.

TAT and Rorschach as well as pressure during interviewing indicate and elicit considerable underlying hostility and anxiety. There is also evidence of an inappropriate naïvete and a rather infantile approach to himself and his place in the world. There is a paucity of general information mainly pertaining to history, geography, sports events, etc. There is, however, indication of a superior I.Q.—a suprisingly good vocabulary and intermittent areas of erudition well beyond the level of a twelve-year-old. There is also evidence of originality and perhaps even of artistry.

Jordi is fearful of contact with his contemporaries, and this can be understood on many levels, among them his great inexperience in this area.

There is evidence of increasing obsessive defensive maneuvers. This is, however, felt to be a good prognostic sign, since the latter is probably a substitute for his earlier autistic existence.

Diagnosis: At this time deferred.

Prognosis: In view of excellent progress, the future looks relatively bright—we hope.

Recommendation: Discharge from this institution within a year. Jordi should then be ready for formal psychoanalytic treatment while attending an ordinary school. We feel that the latter school must be small and provide for individual understanding and attention.

At the time of discharge we will refer Jordi to one of our list of child psychoanalysts, who may then have a conference with our staff and Jordi's teacher.

The Beginning

"Jordi, how do you feel about going to another school?"

"Another school?" he asked, obviously confused. "Will you be there? Will you be there with me, Sally?"

She went on. "Jordi, you don't understand. Do you remember we once talked about more grown-up schools, about high schools and colleges?"

"Yes, I remember, but will you be there, Sally?"

"No, Jordi, I won't be there—but you will learn a great deal more about angles, about history and many interesting things. And there will be other teachers there, and you will meet children your age there too."

"I don't want to go, Sally. I want to stay with you."

"You're not leaving yet, Jordi. It won't be for another six months."

"Do I have to go? Do I have to, Sally? Who will I talk to? Who will tell me I'm Jordi if I get lost—who, Sally?"

He began to cry, and she hugged him to her.

"You won't get lost, Jordi. You're lots better now. Your problem hardly shows anymore—that's why you don't have to stay. You can go to a regular school."

"You mean Lisa can't leave?" he said through his tears.

"No, she can't leave, Jordi. Besides, Jordi, you will have Dr. Mills to talk to. You will see him every day after school."

"Oh, Sally—oh, why did you tell me, why? Now my problems will show—now mine will show."

"Let them show, Jordi, and cry all you like. And, Jordi," she said, "you will visit me. You can come now and then, and I'll come and see you at home every few months. We can talk on the phone too."

"Everything hurts. Please, please, don't say any more, Sally."

But Sally said much more. They talked and talked about his departure from the school.

And then only two days remained before Jordi would leave. Four and a half years had passed since he entered the "ice house."

"Jordi, in two days you will go to your new school, but remember you can visit here."

He suddenly swirled about, faced her, and yelled, "You hate me, you hate me. You lied, you lied. You never liked me never. And I hate you, I hate you."

He picked up a blackboard eraser and threw it, shattering the nearest window.

Then he ran out of the room and out of the building. He just ran and ran, too dazed to think or watch where he was going. But he soon found himself on the subway and in the front car of the Lexington Avenue express.

He rode all over New York and cried most of the time. Then he thought about Sally and the times gone by. Then he thought about their talks of the last six months.

When he got back, it was six o'clock, but everybody was still there. Even his mother and father were there.

Then he saw her, and she said, "Jordi, I'm so glad to see you. I'm so glad to see you, Jordi."

He looked at her and said, "I came back, I came back. Sally, I came back to leave."

Other books by Dr. Theodore Isaac Rubin are available at your local bookstore or by mail. To order directly, return the coupon below to Macmillan Publishing Company, Special Sales Department, 866 Third Avenue, New York, NY 10022.

Line Sequence	ISBN	Title	Price	Quantity
1	0-02-077820-1	THE ANGRY BOOK	$4.95	——
2	0-02-077750-7	COMPASSION AND SELF-HATE	$4.95	——
3	0-02-053580-5	JORDI	$3.95	——
4	0-02-053570-8	LISA AND DAVID	$3.95	——
5	0-02-077800-7	THE WINNER'S NOTEBOOK	$4.95	——

Subtotal ——

Please add postage and handling costs—$1.00 for the first book and 50¢ for each additional book

Sales tax—if applicable ——

TOTAL ——

—— Enclosed is my check/money order payable to Macmillan Publishing Company.

—— Bill my —— MasterCard —— Visa Card # _____ Control No. _____ Ord. Type REG

Expiration date _____ Signature _____ For charge orders only:

Charge orders valid only with signature

Ship to: _____ Bill to: _____

_____ Zip Code _____ Zip Code

Lines Units
☐
☐

For information regarding bulk purchases, please write to Special Sales Director at the above address. Publisher's prices are subject to change without notice. Allow 3 weeks for delivery.

FC # 273